Wessex F

C000299449

Contents

The Time of Their Lives

The last great rebellions by Englishmen took place in the area of the south-west historically known as Wessex. The Duke of Monmouth, a bastard son of Charles II, relied on the stubborn independent spirit of many of the yeomen farmers and middling folk and their communities. 'For these peasant followers of Monmouth, the dark Puritan faith glowed in all the colours of personal romance; they loved the young man more than they loved their lives. Of Monmouth, as of Napoleon, tales were told at nightfall beneath the thatch, and his return was still expected long after he was dead.' But he was a pied piper who led them to disaster.

For William, Prince of Orange, Wessex contained one of two accessible areas considered for landing, at a sufficient distance from the bases of the substantial army of King James II. A 'protestant' east wind sprang up and drove William's great fleet westward settling the matter of its destination.

Charles II, Monmouth and James II all knew deprivation and exile in their time, and William III felt himself a solitary and neglected child; conflict and political upheaval never ceased to disturb their adult days, but Western Europe was advancing, building its empires, giving birth to painters, musicians, horticulturalists, engineers and learning how to make money work through new capitalist institutions.

William's Dutch fleet setting sail for England.

Nature as well as man was determined to be reckoned with; in general the summers were arid and the winters often ferocious.

Great Frost Fairs could be held on the deep, strong ice of the Thames:

> '. . . *the very seas locked up with ice so that no vessels could stir out or come in. The fowls, fish and birds and all our exotic plants and greens universally perishing. Many packs of deer destroyed, and all sorts of fuel so dear that there were contributions to preserve the poor alive . . . London was so filled with the fuliginous steam of sea coal that hardly could one see across the streets; and this filling the lungs with its gross particles exceedingly obstructed the breath . . . There was no water to be had from the pipes and engines; nor could the brewers and divers other tradesmen work . . .*'
>
> JOHN EVELYN, *Diary*, 1683–4

The Frozen Thames, *1667, detail, by A. Hondius. In 1676–7 and 1684 ice fairs were held on the Thames.*

King Charles II engraving.

Powerful storms frequently affected historical events of these times from the 'mercy' which destroyed the Spanish Armada in 1588 to that which delayed and nearly confounded the invasion fleet of William of Orange.

Bitter days when rivers and even the sea were frozen encouraged a diet which caused the Italians to dub us 'Carnivorous England'. Plates were heaped high with mutton, salt beef, rabbit, pigeon and fowl, supported by mounds of cabbage and turnip, often smothered with butter. A fish diet was observed in Lent and strawberries and other fruit had been grown in farm-gardens for a century. This was a thirst-making diet and our copious draughts of beer, and wine for the wealthier, began to be joined by coffee, and coffee houses became urban political and social centres. Tea, regarded in Holland as a beneficial luxury, also became popular here. A 'Frenchified' Court began to demand a cuisine with more subtle recipes, but these were not for Wessex yeomen.

Hygiene was mostly ignored and the terror of plague lingered long after the last great epidemic of 1665. Other diseases – 'flu, smallpox and typhus – were recurrent. Medicine was making progress; the first dentists as opposed to crude tooth-pullers made their appearance. Harvey had taught us about the circulation of the blood and in 1660 the Royal Society had received its charter.

Dorset has a worse memory of the Great Plague. It was carried to Poole . . . by goods contained in a pedlar's pack. The Magistrates were able to stamp out the pestilence by removing the sick to a pest-house at a distance from the town. They had difficulty in finding anyone to serve as nurse . . . and had resort to engaging a young woman then . . . in gaol under sentence of death, on a promise . . . to use their influence to secure a pardon. The nurse performed her risky duty and escaped infection and quickly after the pest-house emptied she was barbarously hanged by the Mayor.

The Great Plague in London
WALTER GEORGE BELL
Folio Society 2000

The Last of the Stuarts

CHARLES I m Henrietta Maria
1600–1649   1609–69

CHARLES II m Catherine of   Mary m William II
1630–85   Braganza d1705   1631–60   Prince of Orange
                                                        d1650

liaison with Lucy
Walter d1658

James Duke of Monmouth   WILLIAM III m MARY II
and Buccleuch 1649–85   1650–1702   1662–74

CHARLES II had fourteen children including, in addition to Monmouth, the Duke of St Albans, child of Nell Gwynn, the Dukes of Southampton, Northumberland and Grafton, children by Barbara Palmer, Countess of Castlemaine and the Duke of Richmond and Lennox by Louise de Kerouaille, Duchess of Portsmouth

In 1686 the population of England was probably a little over five million; about one million lived in the six south-western counties of Cornwall, Devon, Somerset, Gloucestershire, Wiltshire and Dorset with 450,000 dwelling in Devon and Somerset.

In the same period about 50,000 refugees, many Huguenots, joined the population bringing new skills and naturally reinforcing anti-Catholic feeling.

Our maritime skills and adventures became more rewarding with the encouragement of rulers like Charles and James who were passionately enthusiastic sailors when opportunity arose, and with the coming of a new breed of full-time professional naval men administered by the indomitable Samuel Pepys. Nevertheless, it is surprising to recall that the fleets and ships of the Barbary Pirates of the North African coast impudently plundered shipping around our shores and sometimes abducted hostages from the land itself, carrying them back to Algiers or Sallee as slaves. The position was not helped when Britain was forced to abandon in 1684 the fortress of Tangier which it had acquired through Charles' marriage to Catherine of Braganza.

A permanent standing army was first created by Charles II at his Restoration; it combined horse and foot guards from both Royalist and Parliamentary forces as a gesture of reconciliation. James II expanded the Army under royal prerogative and it was the fear and dissension which this created which ensured that the Declaration of Rights under William provided that without the authority of Parliament the raising of an army would be illegal.

King James II

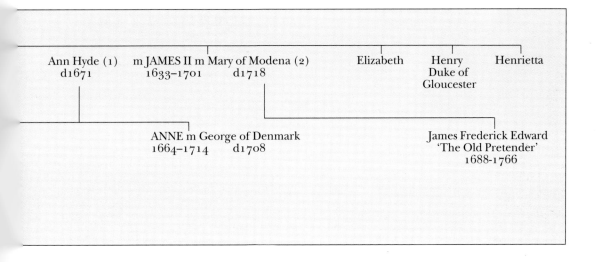

Monmouth – a love child

The Duke of Monmouth

Forde Abbey where Sir Edmund Prideaux entertained the Duke of Monmouth during Monmouth's progress through the West of England. Later it cost Prideaux £15,000 to save himself from the gallows.

James Crofts, later to be James Scott, Duke of Monmouth, Duke of Buccleuch in Scotland, Earl of Dalkeith, Baron Tynedale, Master of the Horse, Chief Justice in Eyre and Chancellor of the University of Cambridge, led the Monmouth rebellion against his uncle James II in 1685. Monmouth was 'the natural son of . . . Charles II and Lucy Walter, a lady of notorious character.'

Monmouth was born in Liège in 1649 when his father was in exile and the fact or otherwise of his legitimacy must colour attitudes to his actions.

Charles himself who had 'overflowing fondness' for this charismatic son, nevertheless was adamant that he had been born out of wedlock. When James II succeeded his brother as king his Catholicism and clumsy and inflexible political stance enraged the Country (Whig) Party. Monmouth had already become nominal head of the Protestant opposition; he was popular with an easy-going manner and had earned a fair reputation as a military tactician and courageous soldier. He became the 'most popular man' in the kingdom and was allowed privileges in the protocol of the Court of Charles given otherwise only to the Duke of York and Prince Rupert, which must have fanned the flames of his ambition and made him think that perhaps the crown itself was not beyond his grasp.

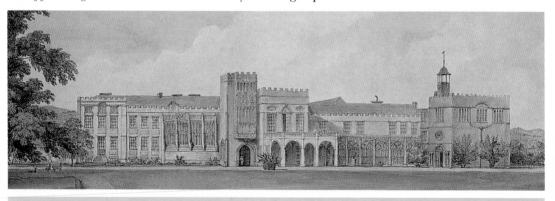

He was a weak, bad and beautiful young man. Though popular, good natured and charming as his reputed father, he had once in a drunken frolic, helped to murder a watchman while the unoffending wretch had begged for mercy on his knees. Monmouth was, perhaps, too light to be accounted criminal. He was born to be the tool of others.

G. M. TREVELYAN *England Under the Stuarts* 1946

In 1680, five years before the death of Charles, Monmouth had been persuaded to make a 'Progress' through the protestant strongholds and Country Party houses of Wessex, meeting often veterans of the Civil War. From Bath through Longleat, Whitelackington House (where a massive crowd of 20,000 people turned out to meet him) and Forde Abbey, he came to Exeter and back again through Ilminster and Clifton Maybank to Longleat.

The starting point for Monmouth's 'Progress' of 1680 was Longleat, home of the Thynne family and Thomas Thynne ('Tom of Ten Thousand'), a generous host and a foremost leader of the country opposition to Court policies. The future of Longleat, which Macaulay described as perhaps the finest house in England, might have been at risk but for the assassination of Thomas Thynne before Monmouth's rebellion, a death which deprived Monmouth of one of his principal influential supporters but averted Longleat from being attainted as a nest of traitors. Thynne was shot with a blunderbuss while travelling in a coach in Pall Mall, the culmination of an eccentric and violent dispute with a Swedish nobleman over the hand of a fifteen-year-old widow heiress. She had been bullied into a second marriage with Thynne by her despotic grandmother, the Countess of Northumberland, with the approval of Thynne's friend Monmouth. The Whig party at first averred that the death was a botched attempt to slay Monmouth himself who had shortly before left the coach in question.

Longleat, built in the sixteenth century, home to the Thynne family for 450 years. 'Perhaps the finest house in England.'
MACAULAY

Whitelackington Manor House by W.W. Wheatley.

At Whitelackington a woman whose hand was infected with the skin disease scrofula had removed her glove and was cured apparently by the touch of the hand of Monmouth. Scrofula was known as the King's Evil, and the credulous locals and the more sophisticated denizens of London coffee houses regarded (or preferred to regard) this as a confirmation of Monmouth's claims to royal legitimacy.

'The Duke had thus shown himself to the people of the West-country. They could have been in no doubt . . . that his purpose was plainly political – to gain support for his cause in an area where Nonconformists were strong for a policy of excluding the Catholic Duke of York from the throne.'

The counties of Wiltshire, Somerset and Devon through which Monmouth had journeyed were not areas of rural backwardness; they were well populated with a large export market for their woollen cloths but this industry was labour-intensive and depended on a 'multitude of laborious poor'.

There followed a period of plots and allegations of plots. The vile Titus Oates had accused the Catholics of a 'popish plot' to kill the King and Monmouth, and although he was a double-dyed villain and clearly a liar, Oates' accusations provoked widespread anti-Catholic hysteria. On the other side the Duke of York was able to make capital from the Rye House plot, a vaguely conceived and unthought through plan to assassinate the King and York. In the prosecutions which followed Rye House, Monmouth refused to give evidence when some of his friends were brought to trial and he was banished, travelling to Brussels in November 1683. Charles had acknowledged and was generous to his bastard sons but he was adamant in maintaining the legitimate succession to the throne. On his deathbed Monmouth's name was omitted from those for whom he asked his brother's favour and protection.

'For a year Monmouth paced Holland like a caged beast – and plot followed plot and scheme followed scheme as he sought ways to regain his former glory.' Then on 5 February 1685 Charles II died and the Duke of York swiftly established himself as king. Monmouth knew that he was probably in danger and certainly it was now or never if he was to achieve his ambitions.

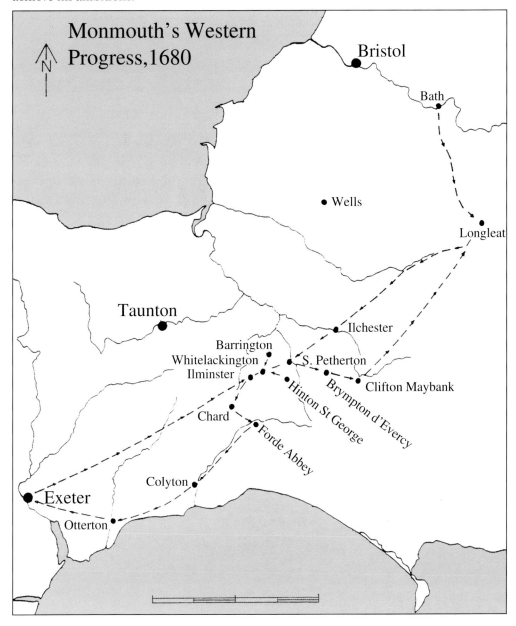

Monmouth's Western Progress, 1680

The Course of the Rebellion

At Lyme Regis, on 11 June 1685, 'It was suddenly observed that three strange ships were approaching the harbour and the Town Surveyor was sent out in a boat to investigate. But after the lapse of a reasonable amount of time he had not returned, and suspicions were aroused. Meanwhile, the vessels were drawing in close to the shore, presumably to avoid the attentions of the forts. The alarm of the townsfolk naturally increased and a party was sent to find ammunition for the guns. The English, however, seem to have a habit of being caught off balance in the early stages of a crisis and so it is not surprising '. . . that no gunpowder could be found . . . .'

'By this time a party of about eighty men had landed on the beach and one of them, obviously a person of some consequence, fell to his knees and kissed the ground. This was, indeed, the Duke of Monmouth on the first stage of his attempt to seize the crown of England from his uncle.'

A Portrait of Lyme, HENRY CHESSEL, 1969

Prospect of Lyme 21 Aug. 1723.
LONDINIS.

A. *Where the Duke of Monmouth Landed*
B. *Portland*
C. *The Pier*

Stuksley del:

'Fear nothing but God' was the motto embroidered on Monmouth's banner and freedom to worship in their own fashion was the most immediate imperative for many of those who rallied to his cause. In the last years of Charles II persecution of Nonconformists had become severer and with an avowed Catholic on the throne their prospects were threatened. Of the small number of competent soldiers in his rebel army, men like Abraham Holmes, who was once a major under General Monk, and Nathaniel Wade, son of a Cromwellian major, were associated with the Puritan days of the Commonwealth. Within a few days a force about 3,000 strong had gathered to the Duke, and under the command of Lord Grey it made its way across the hills to Taunton where his agents had been meeting and waiting for news at the 'Red Lion'.

A playing card shows Monmouth leading his men into Lyme.

Gun Cliff fort in Lyme Regis.

Taunton, a town of staunch puritan sympathies, had been held for Parliament throughout the Civil War, and supported an academy for young ladies from families often of 'ample wealth and Whig leanings'. When Monmouth's army arrived in Taunton on 18 June 1685, the townsfolk wore sprigs of leveller green which reminds us that for most of the Westcountry folk it was freedom of religion rather than changes of monarchy which prompted their zeal, and the shouts were for 'A Monmouth and the Protestant Religion!'.

There occurred an incident of curious charm but which was the occasion later of a sinister tragedy. The town greeted the rebels with rejoicing, and the girls of the school had been embroidering from their own silk petticoats, 27 banners for the rebel regiments, although why in that prosperous place it was necessary for the maidens to sacrifice their undergarments is unclear! Led by their two mistresses and escorted by soldiers they proceeded in crocodile, at their head Miss Mary Blake carrying a Bible and a sword which she presented to the Duke, who responded: 'I have come into the field to defend the truths contained in this book and to seal them if it must be with my blood.' One of the banners fringed and embroidered in gold, bore a crown and the letters JR-Jacobus Rex. This inscription obviously honoured King (James Scott) Monmouth and not his uncle James II in London, and was the first clear indication that Monmouth asserted his right to the crown, a treason for which he could expect no mercy if he

Taunton Castle,
by Harry Frier, 1898.

failed. On 20 June the arguments of Lord Grey and the evil plotter Ferguson prevailed over the opposition of the old (and wiser) republicans in his following, and in the market place it was proclaimed: 'For the deliverance of the Kingdom from popery, tyranny and oppression [we] do recognise, publish and proclaim the said high and mighty Prince, James, Duke of Monmouth, our lawful and rightful sovereign and King, by the name of James the Second.'

After Monmouth's defeat 'some of the girls who had presented the standard to Monmouth at

Taunton had cruelly expiated their offence. One of them had been thrown into a prison where an infectious malady was raging. She had sickened and died there. Another had presented herself at the bar before Jeffreys to beg for mercy.

'Take her, gaoler,' vociferated the judge, with one of those frowns which had often struck terror into stouter hearts than hers. She burst into tears, drew her hood over her face, followed the gaoler out of court, fell ill of fright, and in a few hours was a corpse. Most of the young ladies, however, who had walked in the procession, were still alive. Some of them were under ten years of age. All had acted under the orders of their schoolmistress, without knowing that they were committing a crime. The Queen's maids of honour asked the royal permission to wring money out of the parents of the poor children; and the permission was granted. An order was sent down to Taunton that all these little girls should be seized and imprisoned. Sir Francis Warre of Hestercomb, the Tory member for Bridgwater, was requested to undertake the office of exacting the ransom. He was charged to declare in strong language that the maids of honour would not endure delay, that they were determined to prosecute to outlawry, unless a reasonable sum were forthcoming, and that by a reasonable sum was meant several thousand pounds. Warre excused himself from taking any part in a transaction so scandalous. The maids of honour then requested William Penn to act for them; and Penn accepted the commission. Yet it should seem that a little of the pertinacious scrupulosity which he had often shown about taking off his hat would not have been altogether out of place on this occasion. He probably silenced the remonstrances of his conscience by repeating to himself that none of the money which he extorted would go into his own pocket; that if he refused to be the agent of the ladies they would find agents less humane; that by complying he should increase his influence at the court, and that his influence at the court had already enabled him, and might still enable him, to render great services to his oppressed brethren. The maids of honour were at last forced to content themselves with less than a third part of what they had demanded' (LORD MACAULAY).

A playing card showing the Duke of Monmouth receiving the colours of the Maids of Taunton.

By the 21st the rebel army now 8,000 strong and in high spirits moved to Bridgwater. On the road from Lyme to Taunton they had routed the local militia sent to oppose them and they were full of confidence. But Monmouth was a battle-tried professional soldier and despite his intellectual limitations he must have known full well that the failure of most of the nobility and local gentry to rally to his cause, and with no defections from James II's regular army, the scales were heavily weighted against his success.

James II had appointed the elderly Earl of Feversham (a naturalised Frenchman, a nephew of Marshal Turenne) to co-ordinate moving against the rebels. John Churchill, later the first Duke of Marlborough, was in the van of the army's deployment westward; he had earlier served under Monmouth in conflicts in Tangier and Flanders, and, later, it was partly his defection to William III which ensured the overthrow of James II. But now he was able and energetic for his royal master.

Monmouth's men were not just an illiterate rabble but extant records suggest chiefly middling sort of folk – clothworkers, yeomen,

various tradesmen and Mendip miners (the last group sustained the heaviest casualties in the conflict). Daniel Defoe who was for a time one of their number confirms this picture of their composition. Nevertheless, as they marched cheerily through a welcoming Bridgwater and on towards Bristol and Bath, these indifferently armed and untrained civilians, without the support of either artillery or a disciplined cavalry arm were doomed. Monmouth, blocked by Feversham's royal forces when close to Bristol, then called on Bath to surrender to him, but the threat was hollow – 'only in bravado, for we had no expectation of its surrender' as Nathaniel Wade recorded.

Although a brush with royalists commanded by his half-brother Grafton ended in a minor rebel victory, Monmouth had to fall back to Norton St Philip. With news of an amnesty offered by James II being discussed in the ranks and his own spirits, with the report of the capture of Argyll, his ally in Scotland, inducing a nervous paralysis, at a council of war Monmouth was prepared to abandon the enterprise but was persuaded by his friends (as so often unwisely he was) to ignore the omens and press on.

Press on – but where to? To Frome they went; finding no promised reinforcements there they turned towards Shepton Mallet. At 'Monmouth's Oak' at Downhead they were augmented by a body of Mendip lead miners of whom John Evelyn reported when the tragedy was over: 'did great execution with their tools and sold their lives very dearly'. Just above Downhead is the hamlet of Soho, named it is thought because it was a vantage point for Monmouth whose rallying cry 'Soho' was taken from Soho Square where his London residence lay.

Uncertain now of their strategy the rebels wandered about Somerset eventually arriving back in Bridgwater on 3 July. Two days later Feversham and Churchill with 2,000 regulars and 1,500 Wiltshire militia camped on Sedgemoor three miles away.

One who is centre-stage in many of the dramas recorded in these pages is the brilliant, brave and devious John Churchill, to be the first and famous Duke of Marlborough. 'He retained courtly characteristics throughout his life, notably the practice of dissimulation. By iron self-control he invariably succeeded in concealing his inner feelings.

An exhausted rebel fleeing the battlefield leans on the table while a fearful cottager listens for sounds of the King's soldiers.

Despite constant stress and frequent provocations he maintained a courteous and affable manner.' Born at Great Trill, Axminster in Devon in 1650, the son of a penniless cavalier, he became a page to the Duke of York and ensign in the Foot Guards; when he was 17 his sister Arabella became acknowledged mistress to James II. He fought early in an English regiment in the French service under the command of Marshal Turenne. When he was 35 it was his drive and experience rather than that of the nominal commander of James II's forces, the Earl of Feversham, which ensured that Monmouth's rebellion collapsed on the flats of Sedgemoor. ('I see plainly that the trouble is mine and that the honour will be another's.')

Ironically, it was Monmouth who had recommended Churchill for his first promotion: the social connections between Monmouth and Grey on one side and Feversham, Churchill and Kirke on the other were close – 'they all came from the same world'. At the news of Monmouth's landing, Churchill, now with the rank of brigadier had led the van of the royal forces west to Salisbury. Nevertheless, Churchill was already unhappy with James II's religious policies and also with the man himself – 'this marble is not harder than the King,' he said when agreeing to intercede, without much hope of success, for rebel prisoners.

Churchill was soon in touch with William of Orange who had a better claim to the succession than the foolish man who had landed at Lyme and ended, inevitably on the block on Tower Hill. When William eventually made his decision to respond to appeals from England and landed at Brixham, he was anxious to avoid a bloody battle which might alienate his future subjects. James, on the other hand, was a courageous and competent military commander and was keen to bring his adversary to battle.

Churchill and a number of prominent figures who had already plotted to betray James were at Salisbury and suggested that their king come to Warminster to inspect his troops. At the time for departure

Blenheim Palace was the magnificent reward bestowed upon John Churchill, the first Duke of Marlborough, by Queen Anne, who succeeded William III as monarch in 1702. Under William, Churchill was for a while stripped of his honours and spent time in the Tower, but he was, in the end, the greatest general in Europe.

James suffered a violent nose-bleed debilitating enough to make him postpone the journey. By the time he was fit enough to hold a council of war the smell of treason was strong in the air and the conspirators were under suspicion although there was no evidence against them; the king's confidence ebbed and he decided on retreat. On the evening of 24 November, Churchill, thinking himself at risk fled with the Duke of Grafton to join William who had reached Axminster. He left behind a fulsome letter acknowledging his indebtedness to his royal master but claiming that: 'he was a protestant and he could not conscientiously draw his sword against the protestant cause'. However sincere this explanation, within three years Churchill became disenchanted with his new master and made tentative overtures to exiled James at the court of St Germains, although had Churchill decided to move against William his real aim would have been to install Anne as queen, counting on his wife Sarah's influence with Anne as her often dominating confidante.

The Battle of Sedgemoor

St Mary's, Bridgwater. From here Monmouth observed the royal forces and made the fatal decison to attack.

The battlefield (opposite), drawn by Michael Stirling.

Sedgemoor Inn still remembers the battle.

From the top of St Mary's, Bridgwater, Monmouth with a spyglass could observe the disposition of the royal troops. He had seen that the royal infantry was not dug in, although as the King later accepted, their position was 'well chosen' and their cavalry ranged the moor; nevertheless Feversham was uncertain of Monmouth's intentions and thought he might try to slip his clutches and head for Bristol. Many and widely-varying estimates have been made of the numbers of men available on either side but it is probable that at this juncture the rebels outnumbered the regular troops opposing them.

Monmouth decided to hazard his fortune now in battle; at 11 p.m. on Sunday 5 July he led his army in silence 'without a drumbeat' towards his enemies. Although the rebels passed within half a mile of Chedzoy village and were observed by two villagers, the king's men were not alerted 'from country dullness and slowness'. A guide had led the rebels successfully until the Langmoor Rhine where they were delayed in locating the crossing point. A pistol shot here – it is said from a Captain Hucker – was the turning point of this melancholy affair. Before the cavalry under Lord Grey whose orders were to

FLAT HOLM

STEEP HOLM

THE MENDIPS

BREAN DOWN

M5

A38

BRENT KNOLL

STERT POINT

BURNHAM

HIGHBRIDGE

CLYCE
c.AD 1485

RIVER BRUE

22

RIVER AXE

WEDMORE

WOOKE

c. AD 878

COMBWICH

A38

M5

MARK MOOR

HUNTSPILL RIVER

MEARE LAKE

The Vale of Avalon

A39

EDINGTON AD 878

POLDEN HILLS

A39

A361

CREINTON

DUNBALL CLYCE

23

R.PARRETT COURSE UP TO 1677

WEST MOOR

KING'S SEDGE

KING'S SEDGEMOOR RHINE 1795

GREYLAKE FOSSE 1510

MOOR

BUTLEIGH MOOR

SOMERTON MOOR

RIVER CARY

BRIDGWATER

A38

M5

24

CANAL

HAY MOOR

A372

WESTONZOYLAND 1685

SOUTH MOOR

LAKE WALL

WESTON LEVEL

MIDDLEZOY

OTHERY

NETHER MOOR

PATHE

BEER WALL 1320

A372

R.CARY 1795

NORTH MOOR

TURN HILL

HIGH HAM

ALLER

NORTH MOOR

EARLAKE MOOR

BURROW MUMP

SOUTH LAKE MOOR

RIVER CARY OLD COURSE

ALLER MOOR

SALTMOOR

RIVER TONE (UP TO 1374)

A361

ATHELNEY

BALT MOOR WALL

STAN MOOR

STATHE

RIVER PARRETT

RIVER SOWY c.1980

OATH LOCK

SEDGEMOOR RHINE

STOKE ST. GREGORY

WEST SEDGE MOOR

HITCHINGS

LYNG

CURLOAD

RIVER TONE (FROM 1374)

RAILWAY

The Somerset Levels

N

CURRY MOOR

CURRY MOOR

NOT TO

A playing card showing rebels looting in Wells.

The roads to and from Sedgemoor. The path of Monmouth's melancholy rebellion.

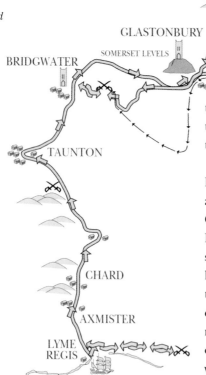

outflank the enemy and fall on his rear, had splashed through the water, a trooper had been sent down the royal lines shouting: 'beat your drums, the enemy is coming'. Grey's cavalry moved forward following their orders, but halted sharply by a further water obstacle, the Bussex Rhine, an obstacle of which Grey had not been warned and of whose depth and character he had no knowledge. He decided to swing south-west along the north side of the rhine and in front of the royal army. Although Grey had turned bravely if unwisely (he was an incompetent soldier if not the coward which is sometimes alleged), towards the enemy his unseasoned horses were quickly panicked and fled north from the field, causing confusion in the ranks of their infantry who were moving up behind them.

Nathaniel Wade with Monmouth's Red Regiment of foot maintained a disciplined advance, despite the confusion caused by Grey's scattered cavalry. As they came opposite Dumbarton's regiment of Scots on the other side of the Bussex Rhine they achieved some lethal execution with the three cannon which they had, but their muskets offered only the ill-disciplined fire of men new to arms whilst the regular soldiers opposite replied with the ordered volleys of trained men. Wade's men were the best led and most courageous of Monmouth's army but once they had halted they refused to advance across the Stygian uncertainties of the ditch before them; Monmouth could see Dumbarton's regiment which he had himself led at the battle of Bothwell Brig and said ruefully: 'If I had had but them, all would be well'.

Soon James's men were reinforced at this point by three royal guns, dragged to the line by the carriage horses of Bishop Mews, and their case-shot (canisters of musket balls) scythed through the rebel ranks. Feversham, the King's commander-in-chief had now belatedly risen from his camp bed and endorsed the orders already given by Churchill for a counter-attack at daylight; the Horse Guards were to pass over the Lower Plungeon (crossing) to deal with Wade, and the Blues were to take the Upper Plungeon. At the first streaks of grey dawn large numbers of rebel scythemen behind Wade were still not engaged, but time had run out for Monmouth. As the cavalry thundered down on the rebels' either flank the foot were ordered over the rhine which they crossed with a great shout of challenge. Wade bowed to the inevitable and ordered a retreat; to Grey who rode up to him Monmouth said: 'Nothing will stop these fellows; they will run presently.' He removed his armour and with Grey and others he rode north into the Mendips taking shelter at Downside, the home of Edward Strode. Monmouth had fought bravely in the battle but surely now he should have stayed with those men who for no reward had given him their allegiance and had been valiant for the truths in which they believed.

Weary rebel troopers and horses trail dejectedly from their defeat at Sedgemoor.

Flight, Capture and Execution

NATHANIAL WADE at Windsor Castle, October 4, 1685

I came acquainted with Colonel John Romsey at an election of Parliament men to serve in the late King's reign for the City of Bristol to which City the Colonel came upon that occasion, and by this means I became known to my Lord Shaftesbury, the Duke of Monmouth and consequently to several gentlemen of that party as Mr West, Goodenough, Mr John Trenchard and others. But my chiefest intimacy was with Col Romsey who always brought messages to me from my Lord Shaftesbury, and gave me an account as often as my Lord had a mind to speak with me.

It was after the Dissolution of the Parliament at Oxford that I first heard of any discourse about having recourse to Arms, it was in Trinity Term next after that Dissolution when Col Romsey coming to my Chambers in the Middle Temple told me that there was an insurrection designed at Taunton . . . and that it was expected by Lord Shaftesbury that I should take a part there which I did not absolutely deny, but being a thing new to me, made some hesitation thereof.

The open country of the Cranbourne Chase, near Woodyates Inn. Monmouth's followers would have found it difficult to navigate a route here.

As Monmouth fled from defeat a babel of siren voices put forward conflicting plans for escape. One was for commandeering a passage boat at Uphill near Weston, and making for Wales, keeping to concealed woodland through Somerset; but the most persuasive voice was that of Lord Grey, who was never a harbinger of good fortune for the rebellion. After refreshment at Downside, Monmouth, Grey and a Brandenburger officer Anton Buyse, at Grey's insistence turned their horses towards the port of Lymington (or Poole where in happier days Monmouth and his father had been handsomely entertained on a visit). They entered Dorset near Berwick St John and reached by way of Cranbourne Chase the then Woodyates Inn. Here they left their horses to traverse on foot the wild country which then lay between them and the south coast, separating for greater safety.

At 5 a.m. on 7 July a patrol of the Sussex militia under Lord Lumley, scouting the edge of the New Forest, stumbled on Grey (who was

known to Lumley) and a guide. A local cottager perhaps spurred to observation by the reward of the huge sum of £5,000 offered for the capture of Monmouth reported seeing two men lurking in nearby smallholdings. After sunrise Buyse was taken and a little later a militiaman named Parkin spotted the skirt of a brown coat among the luxuriant ferns and brambles of a ditch.

'He clutched at it, and found . . . the palpitating body of a man, terror-stricken and trembling . . . This haggard, ragged hatless wretch was Monmouth . . . He was in the dress of a farm hand but in the pockets of his coat were found things which were never before discovered in the pockets of a Dorset shepherd. These were the Badge of the Order of the Garter, recipes for cosmetics, forecasts from astrologers and numerous quaint charms to ward off evil.' Also, around his neck a woman's blue ribbon, fastened with a silver buckle, very likely a keepsake from his mistress, Lady Henrietta Wentworth, to whom he showed more sustained loyalty than to any other man or woman.

July 29 1685, Confession made by Nicholas Wade to Henry Clavering

Monmouth expected Sir Walter Young, Sir Francis Rolle of Hampshire and other gentlemen, but they all failing him made him grow very melancolly, his intent was for Bristoll being persuaded by Capt Tily that most of the citizens were for him and then for Glo'ster & so to London, this is all he can do at present but he will declare all he knows as soon as he is able being desperately wounded by a pistol shot almost thro' his body.

Hardwick State Papers Vol II (1778), pp 305–314 (ff 289–296), pp 315–332 (ff 274–282)

Monmouth, found in a ditch.

Background
The Monmouth Oak.

The excitable militiamen would fain have shot their prize out of hand but he was rescued from this danger and taken in an exhausted state to Ringwood by those who felt that respect was due to a King's son, even one heading for the scaffold. Monmouth had a heavy cold and Grey, who had rejoined them, jested that if the cold still troubled him King James had a ready cure.

Why Grey was so mirthful and how Monmouth who was lapsing into a deep and bitter depression responded, one can only conjecture. At Ringwood Monmouth lodged at a house in West Stret, now called Monmouth House. The pitiful letters which Monmouth penned in the two nights he was here – to the King, Charles II's widow Queen Catherine and others '. . . were abject, unbelievable and useless as his act of high treason made his doom inevitable. '. . . My misfortune was such as to meet some horrid people that made me believe things of Your Majesty, and gave me so many false arguments, that I was led to believe it was a shame and a sin against God not to do it.' The broken-spirited man was taken via Winchester and Guildford to London and by a King's barge to the Tower. Here already incarcerated were his wife and children, but his meeting with them was cold. At the day of his execution there were at the scaffold Ken, Bishop of Bath and Wells, the Bishop of Ely, George Hooper and, at the Duke's request, Dr Thomas Tenison. Monmouth had signed a paper admitting his illegitimacy but stubbornly denied that his had been an act of rebellion and vehemently maintained that his mistress, Lady Henrietta Wentworth, was his 'wife before God'.

The appalling climax of this tragedy was that the executioner botched the beheading, taking five strokes of the axe and the use of a knife to finish the job, a gory horror which infuriated the watching crowds. And what of Lord Grey, second most important figure in the rebellion? He like Monmouth was indubitably guilty, he like Monmouth had secured an audience with the King but unlike his leader he was pardoned. His large estates could be made profitable for his captors. In the event he had to pay a bond of £40,000 to the Lord Treasurer and lived on to become Earl of Tankerville and a leading politician in the reign of William III. Unfortunately, in revolutions trimmers with a gift of cunning often prosper.

Bloody Aftermath

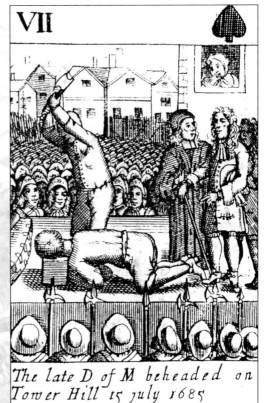

The late D of M beheaded on Tower Hill 15 July 1685

The retribution exacted after the rebellion on the rebels and their helpers included the hideous punishment of hanging, drawing and quartering, with one Somerset man acquiring the soubriquet 'Tom Boilman' from his duties in boiling up human joints prior to the public exhibition. The unspeakable cruelty of all this is almost less offensive to the nostrils than the financial transactions involving prisoners, including the little maids of Taunton. Transportation was to be the fate of near 600; they had been allotted to various West Indian magnates, including the Governors of Jamaica and of the Leeward Islands. The 'King anxious like all Stuarts to gratify his friends at the public expense, allocated 849 rebels to the Queen and half-a-dozen deserving courtiers from fifty to two hundred apiece'. Distinctive among prisoners executed was John Kidd, former keeper at Longleat who had been the only man honoured by Monmouth with a dubious 'knighthood' and who was said to have enlisted as many as 500 in the neighbourhood. He was hanged on the beach at Lyme where he had landed with great expectations. Jeffreys has rightly incurred much of the opprobrium for the bloody aftermath but there were others as vicious as he; Colonel Kirke of the Tangier Regiment, 'Kirke's Lambs' is reputed to have slain many prisoners without trial and to have achieved the consent of a Crewkerne innkeeper's daughter to his attentions on the grounds that then her father would be spared; when she awoke in the morning her father's corpse was hanging outside her window.

Blackmore in Lorna Doone has Jan Ridd who unwisely visits the battlefield of Sedgemoor, at the point of immediate hanging by Kirke when saved by Jeremy Stickles who avers: 'There is no such thing as a trial here: we hang the good folk without it, which saves them much anxiety.' On the shoulder of each was the hand of the King who was moved generally not by mercy but by revenge or the avarice of his family and courtiers.

His behaviour was beyond anything that was ever heard of in a civilised nation. He was perpetually either drunk or in a rage, more like a fury than the zeal of a judge. He required the prisoners to plead guilty. And in that case he gave them some hope of favour, if they gave him no trouble; otherwise he told them that he would execute the letter of the law upon them in its utmost severity. This made many plead guilty, who had a great defence in law. But he shewed no mercy. He ordered a great many to be hanged up immediately without allowing them a minute's time to say their prayers. England had never known anything like it.

GILBERT BURNET, *one-time Chaplain to King Charles II*

The most disciplined and courageous of Monmouth's officers, Nathianel Wade, did escape punishment. Captured in the combes of Exmoor he was promised a pardon if he revealed the names of fellow consipirators – this he did but somehow managed to mention only those already captured, fled or dead. although James II was sarcastic about his revelations he was set free and lived on to be sometime Mayor of Bristol, a point of light in a deeply melancholy business.

The house in Dorchester in which Jeffreys is said to have conducted his merciless trials. It is now a pleasant coffee shop.

Judge Jeffreys's House, Dorchester

So infamous is the reputation of Judge Jeffreys that, as with Richard III, recent historians have searched desperately for a few facts to extenuate his behaviour; 'no one was that wicked'. Born in Denbighshire in 1648 he had risen to be Chief Justice of the King's Bench by the age of 35, and was dead at 41; whatever cruelties he perpetrated they were those of a youngish man. He presided over the trials of the notorious Titus Oates and others; impartiality was not a pre-requisite for a judge in those times – they were appointed 'per bene placito', 'at the king's pleasure'.

When Jeffreys went on his 'campaign in the west' his naturally brutal disposition, his vicious cross-examinations and foul comments and the fact that he was in pain with gallstones, produced a malevolent inhumanity that overrides any defence that he was only doing his duty to his master and cleansing the country of rebels, although James II implacable and grateful for a bitter revenge on the rebels, appointed Jeffreys Lord Chancellor. At lovely Cothelstone Manor on the fringe of the Quantocks, Sir John Stawell, although a loyal supporter of James, refused to co-operate in Jeffreys' disgusting efforts to extract ransoms for the 'Maids of Taunton'; to teach him a lesson Jeffreys had two prisoners hanged on the gateposts of his Cothelstone home. Unsurprisingly, later we find Stawell's name appended to a document supporting William of Orange.

Macaulay records: 'The hatred in which he (Jeffreys) was regarded by the people of Somersetshire has no parallel in our history . . . long transmitted from generation to generation and raged fiercely against his innocent progeny. When he had been many years dead, his grand-daughter, the Countess of Pomfret, travelling on the western road was insulted by the populace. 'When William landed in England, James appointed Jeffreys one of a council of five to carry on the government in London whilst he went to Salisbury to the army; this did not last long, James's days were numbered and Jeffreys fled but was recognised in Wapping by a man whom he had once tried; his disguise of a sailor begrimed with coal dust availed nothing and in terror he was taken through crowds baying for his life to the safety of the Tower. Before he died there broken by sickness, intemperance and naked fear he was visited by John Tutchin, a man whom Jeffreys at Dorchester had sentenced to be flogged every fortnight for seven years. Tutchin behaved with admirable restraint and dignity when Jeffreys abased himself, offered wine and claimed that he had been 'obeying orders', a claim that can never entirely absolve a man from his individual responsibility for his actions.

The gateway of Cothelstone Manor, from which rebel heads were hung as a warning to others.

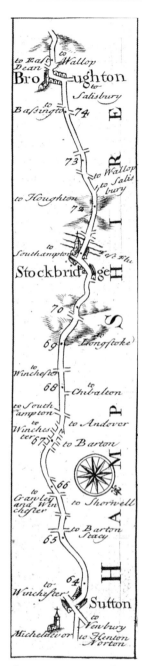

A contemporary map of an area near to Moyles Court.

'The revenge taken by James upon his subjects went far beyond expectation and precedent. . . . He allowed one woman, Alice Lisle, to be beheaded for exercising common charity to fugitives who had implored food and shelter.' G.M. TREVELYAN

The death of Lady Lisle by the axe in the market place (today the Square) at Winchester in the afternoon of 2 September 1685 is one event in the aftermath of Monmouth's rebellion most familiar to readers of history, and is quoted as an exemplar of the vindictive, cruel and illegal work of the abominated Judge Jeffreys.

Lady Lisle who lived at Moyles Court on the western borders of Hampshire was born at that house, the daughter of Sir William Beckenshaw. She was an active nonconformist and widow of John Lisle who had acted for the tribunal which sent Charles I to the scaffold. On the accession of Charles II John Lisle was forced to flee to the Continent but was assassinated in Lausanne in 1664 by an Irish royalist. Alice remained in England with her son and six daughters to endure the taunts of 'Mrs Lisle, the Regicide's wife'.

Among the men who arrived at her house at night for shelter on 28 July 1685, three weeks after the battle of Sedgemoor was Hickes, a fanatical rebel and Presbyterian preacher, but it was an intermediary called Dunne who was brought to Winchester for the trial and was subjected to a remorseless cross-examination by Jeffreys. That prejudices could be absent from the court was unlikely; the arresting officer Thomas Penruddock was the son of Colonel John Penruddock who had been condemned to death by the prisoner's husband in the Commonwealth days after an abortive rebellion.

It was clear that Alice Lisle was aware of the outlawry of the men she harboured but that Jeffreys to secure a conviction was wrong in his direction to the jury regarding the law. As one writer has summarised this melancholy affair: 'The ultimate tragedy is not that, as so many writers have sought to suggest, she was a martyred innocent wrongly convicted but that she was a heroine who was wrongly convicted in spite of her guilt.' A 'merciful' king after intercessions by clergy and nobility ordained that she should not be 'drawn on a hurdle to a place of execution where your body is to be burnt until ye be dead', the prescribed sentence for treason by women. Instead she would be executed by beheading. A contemporary account says 'she was old and dozy, and died without much concern'.

Hollander in Waiting

The 'Dutch' houses on the Strand at Topsham in Devon, built from Dutch bricks used as returning ballast in ships plying the trade, particularly in woollen goods, which developed at the end of the 17th century between the Netherlands and the West of England, have a dignified charm typical of the architecture and art of the period we identify by the names of the joint sovereigns, William and Mary.

It is curious that a man, William of Orange, who led the virtually bloodless 'Glorious Revolution' which ensured that England would be and flourish as a constitutional monarchy with power invested in a free parliament is usually written of with grudging respect rather than enthusiasm. True, the court of Charles II found him a dull dog; 'he did not care for the play, dancing brought on his asthma and he considered gambling a waste of time. What was to be done with such a young man?' Macaulay delineates the future king more fairly; '. . . a slender and feeble frame . . . an eye rivalling that of an eagle . . . a thoughtful and somewhat sullen brow, a firm and somewhat peevish mouth. . . . That pensive, severe and solemn aspect could scarcely have belonged to a happy or a good-humoured man. But it indicates in a manner not to be mistaken capacity equal to the most arduous enterprises and fortitude not shaken by reverses or dangers.'

'Dutch' houses at Topsham, Devon, constructed using materials carried as ballast in voyages from the United Provinces.

He was born with violent passions and quick sensibilities: but the strength of his emotions was not suspected by the world. He praised and reprimanded, rewarded and punished, with the stern tranquillity of a mohawk chief; but those who knew him well were aware that under all this ice a fierce fire was constantly burning.

LORD MACAULAY
History of England
(1889)

'The House in the Wood', one of William and Mary's attractive smaller residences near the Hague.

William III and his fleet approaching Brixham, where they landed.

William III and Mary II by Romeyn de Hooghe (1645–1708).

When he was only twenty-two the states-general of the republic of the United Provinces alarmed by threats from France appointed the young man of promise, captain-general and admiral-general, and a year later he became 'stadtholder', a revived quasi-monarchical office which was made hereditary in 1674. His youthful courage and integrity were rarely in doubt although the murder at this time by an incensed mob of the able John de Witt, Grand Pensionary of Holland, was treated with an aloof indulgence which shadows his biography, as did Glencoe later. In 1674 also peace was concluded with Britain enabling him to marry three years later his cousin Mary. William at times showed friendship to the popular Duke of Monmouth and 'caressed' him to the annoyance of Charles II, but he certainly had no intention of supporting his illegitimate claim to the throne to the detriment of his own self-interest. When Monmouth rose in rebellion William arranged for English and Scots regiments which had been fighting under his command to return to support his father-in-law James II against the attempt to topple him.

At home the tiger-like fierce tenacity of the United Provinces at bay against their enemies was decisive; the dykes were opened and a vast army of 100,000 Frenchmen was impotent against the rising waters and heroic cities as the Spaniards had been in days gone by. William took a cool view of the affairs of Europe; he was not a bigoted anti-Catholic.

Sometimes he would stay at a beguinage in his journeyings, and sometimes he would have the Pope on his side in countering the overweening ambitions of Louis XIV. But at deep centre he was a Protestant and a man of toleration.

This is how William, Prince of Orange, was seen in his own country; powerful, determined and strong.

A contemporary Dutch print of William coming ashore at Brixham. Some English 'wit' ascribed to William the words 'I come to do you goots. I come for all your goots.'

Monmouth had launched his ill-starred attempt on the throne at Lyme Regis with a puny band of followers; when William landed at Brixham further west, three years later on 5 November 1688, he came with the agreement of the authorities in the Netherlands and in a splendid armada, 50 major warships, 26 frigates, 300 merchantmen, pinks and fly-boats, 25 fire ships and 100 Schieveninger fishing boats. A taciturn man of little personal ostentation William may have been, but the nobility, the arms and uniforms, the nationalities from Swiss to Finlanders, and the caparisons of his horsemen were a splendid tribute to the majesty of his office and to the reputation of the greatest protestant soldier of Europe.

The diary of John Whittle, a chaplain with the Prince, left us a full record of the events of the invasion's progress.

William was ambivalent in his relations with James II; his primary concern was the continuing brooding menace of French power and he was anxious to preserve a close friendship with England as a

'By this time the People of Devonshire thereabout had discover'd the Fleet, the one telling the other thereof; they came flocking in droves to the side or brow of the Hills to view us: Some guess'd we were French, because they saw divers white Flags; but the Standard of the Prince, the Motto of which was "For the Protestant Religion and Liberty" soon undeceived them.

'Whereupon all the People shouted for Joy, and Huzza's did now eccho into the Air, many amongst them throwing up their Hats, and all making Signs with their Hands.

'Tis, methinks, impossible for any Man to be so blinded as not to discern the Design of God in this Expedition, from the beginning to the end thereof, for a very favourable wind now fill'd our Sails, and brought us into the long-desired Haven, to the Joy of our Hearts and the Comfort of England.'

An Exact
DIARY
OF THE
Late Expedition
OF
His Illustrious Highness
THE
Prince of Orange,
(Now KING of *Great Britain*)
From his Palace at the *HAGUE,*
To his Landing at *TORBAY;*
And from thence
To his Arrival at *WHITE-HALL.*

Giving a particular ACCOUNT
Of all that happened, and every Day's March.

By a Minister, Chaplain in the ARMY.

LONDON:
Printed for *Richard Baldwin,* near the *Black Bull* in the *Old-Baily.* MDCLXXXIX.

counterweight to French ambitions. James wanted William and Mary to support his repeal of the anti-Catholic Penal and Test Acts. Such a repeal could have resulted in the government of England being increasingly in the hands of Catholic ministers and courtiers, who would have been ready to ally themselves to Louis as the secret diplomacy of Charles II had done in earlier years, to the fury of parliament. Indeed, it was Charles' hope of restoring his own popularity which had encouraged him to endorse the marriage of his niece Mary to his nephew William. By 1688 the stubborn, often stupid actions of James had precipitated calls from the Bishop of London and six leading laymen (the Immortal Seven) and other groups to William to come to protect liberty and property, also to save the claim of Mary to succeed to the throne for it was thought that James II's newborn son in Whitehall Palace later to be the 'Old Pretender', was an impostor.

According to a perhaps suspect tradition William came ashore in a little boat from which he announced: 'Mine people I am come for your goots, I am come for all your goots.' A Mr Youlden sensibly responded for the assembled Devonians:

'Am it please your Majesty, King William,
You'm welcome to Brixham Quay
To eat buckhorn and drink Bohea*
Along o'we.'

*'Bohea' was a poor grade
of tea but tea was generally
an expensive luxury.

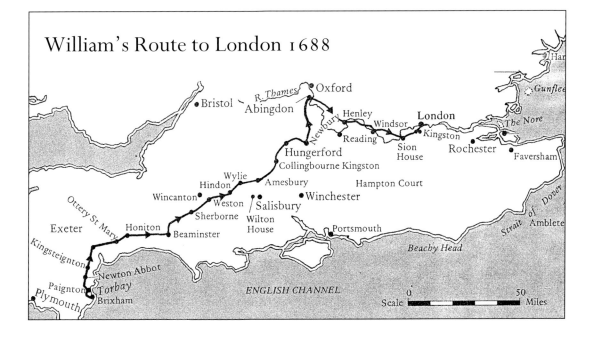

William's Route to London 1688

Brixham obelisk marking the landing of William.

'Parliament' at Longcombe near Totnes, Devon, where 'Gentlemen of the West' agreed to come out for the Prince.

'If I am welcome come and carry me ashore,' said the future king and a Peter Varwell strode to the shore and carried him to dry land on his shoulders. Some versions of the story say that Varwell preceded the prince on his march to London, riding on a small pony and carrying a ring (or favour) given him by William. His reward for this tenacious loyalty on presentation at court was to be the then very handsome sum of 100 guineas but Peter like many before and since soon fell among thieves at the capital and the ring was lost.

William's fleet carried an army of 15,000 men all of whom were landed by 3 o'clock on 6 November, a triumph of organisation, despite some temporary confusion; 'divers jeoparded their lives for haste . . . one or two were over Head and Ears,' the artillery, ammunition and stores were sent by sea to Topsham to avoid the difficult terrain ('full of mountains and rocks') between Brixham and Exeter.

The Ordnance Survey still marks as Parliament the longhouse at Longcombe between Totnes and Newton Abbot where 'gentlemen of the west' who had encouraged William to come over, met under the auspices of Sir Edward Seymour, agreed to 'come out for the Prince' when he reached Exeter. William was entertained by Sir Edward afterwards at his home at Berry Castle.

The late King James at Salisbury

The late King James we heard now was advanc'd as far towards us as Salisbury, with a very brave Army, of about thirty-five thousand Men, and a prodigious great Train of Artillery, which made the poor Country People tremble. Moreover we heard, that he was fully resolved to encamp his Army about Sarum, in the Plain, where he intended to fight us. Some of our Men, being of the Van-guard, were advanc'd as far as Wincaunton to provide Carriage, at which place there was a small Skirmish or Action between 26 of our Souldiers, and about 150 of the late King's Party; which you shall have a particular account by and by. We soon receiv'd information of this skirmish at Exeter: Order was now given to get Waggons to carry the Magazine and Baggage of the whole Army, together with all sorts of Utensils fit and convenient for War, and Horses to draw the Artillery, and for the Country People round to bring in their Horses to be sold at Exeter, that so the loss of our Horses might be made up here: according to which Order the Country People came daily in, with their Horses to sell, and the Officers gave great Prices for them, because they must have them there or nowhere. The Souldiers were ordered to keep themselves and their Arms in good order, and to get every thing here which they wanted. Much Mony was laid out in this City for all sorts of Commodities which the Officers or Souldiers lacked. Here at first the People were scrupulous about the Dutch Mony, and many Country People refused it, but were forc'd to take it, because all the Army had little else, but Guineas and Dutch Mony.

The Prince was received with enthusiasm in Newton Abbot the first market town on his progress, where it was thought appropriate to read a Declaration of his coming: 'for preserving of the Protestant Religion and restoring the Law and Liberties of England, Scotland and Ireland, etc.' For some days the Prince stayed at Forde House as the guest of Sir William Courtney in a room still known as the Orange room. (One citizen had commented, 'if this thing do miscarry we are all undone'. Sir Will, also having some regard to the fate of many who had supported Monmouth, did not remain to greet his guest but arranged to be absent during the days of his residence.)

Berry Pomeroy Castle was abandoned by Sir William, Seymour's son, and it is now 'one of the most romantically beautiful ruins in Devon'.

Forde House, Newton Abbot, a handsome Jacobean mansion.

William's procession included the Earl of Macclesfield with 200 horse, 200 blacks from the Dutch American possessions to attend the horse, 200 Finlanders 'in bearskins taken from the wild beasts they had slain', the Prince on 'a milk-white palfrey', with 42 footmen running after him, 3,000 Switzers with muskets, and on and on . . .

The first of William's adherents to reach Exeter, a Captain Hicks was arrested by the mayor, Sir Thomas Jefford, who also refused to welcome the prince when he arrived on 9 November. This was a very wet and cool day but the flamboyance of William's procession must have lightened the gloom.

Although, the people in general welcomed him warmly the clergy and authorities dithered; at a crowded service in the cathedral as soon as the Prince's Declaration of Intent was read they scuttled away to preserve their neutrality until they could see which way the national wind blew.

William held court in the Deanery and soon doubts about his success dissipated – prominent figures such as Russell, one of the Immortal Seven, came to the city and William was overwhelmed with volunteers from 'the rabble of the people' but his cool assessment of the likely strength and loyalty of James's army enabled him to be selective in his recruitment. On 18 November Lord Bath, a descendant of Bevil Greville, a renowned Cavalier commander in the Civil War, wrote from Plymouth to declare his and the port's allegiance to the Prince, and Colonel Luttrell, whose loyalties in the Monmouth rebellion had been ambiguous, rode in from Dunster Castle to join in.

Dunster Castle

By the time William left Exeter on 20 November to move towards Salisbury he could feel a growing confidence. The Reverend Whittle's Diary states: 'I suppose our Army was now in

Circumference between 20 and 30 miles,' and the troops trudged on despite atrocious rain and mud. At Honiton the Prince stayed at the Dolphin Inn whose sign was taken from part of the crest of the Courtenay family who owned it. At Axminster he slept and dined at Coaxdon Hall, grumbling that his favourite Dutch beer had been contaminated by sea water.

For two nights he slept at the 16th century home of the Paulett family at Hinton St George and for three days at Sherborne. Further halts were made at Wincanton and at Hindon, where William received his first overtures from James suggesting negotiations. As they moved inexorably forward the weather improved and morale was high as Macaulay described.

James had been a courageous and able military and naval commander and at first had been eager for battle, but William wanted no bloody conflict as he advanced to take the keys of the kingdom. The smell of treachery hung in the air round James at Salisbury. Kirke and other officers were already on the way to the Prince and his army's morale was low and the desire to fight swiftly turned into a decision to retreat. Two days after James headed back from Salisbury his other daughter, Princess Anne, accompanied and advised by Sarah Churchill, wife of John Churchill, deserted her father and fled from London to Nottingham.

'. . . the invaders . . . were within seventy miles of London. Though midwinter was approaching, the weather was fine; the way was pleasant; and the turf of Salisbury Plain seemed luxuriously smooth to men who had been toiling through the miry ruts of the Devonshire and Somerset highways. The route of the army lay close by Stonehenge: and regiment after regiment halted to examine that mysterious ruin . . . William entered Salisbury with military pomp (after a detour to see the Van Dyck paintings at Wilton), and was lodged there in the palace which the king had occupied a few days before.'

LORD MACAULAY

The Bear at Hungerford.

On 6 December William arrived at the 'Bear' at Hungerford, a venerable inn which as a hospice 'le Bere' figured in the marriage settlement of Henry VIII's wife Anne of Cleeves. Here came Commissioners from King James to negotiate for a resolution of the great dispute; they were received with dignity and a guard of honour and brought proposals for parliament to arbitrate and for William's army to halt its advance at least forty miles from London. William expressed some surprise that the proposals were presented in French since all previous correspondence between William and his father-in-law had been in English, although French was the language of William's court. Later the Prince retired to the mansion of Littlecote where a splendid assembly gathered to hear William's restrained and courteous reply which sought to hold together the multitude of opinions of the spectrum of his Whig and Tory (old cavalier) supporters. The heart of the matter was reached when Lord Halifax (one of those who had written earlier to the Prince indicating that England's salvation might one day lie in his hands), for James asked: 'Do you want to get the King into your power?' 'Not at all,' said Bishop

Burnet; 'we would not do the least harm to his person.' 'And if he were to go away?' questioned Halifax. 'There is nothing,' said Burnet, 'so much to be wished.' The outcome of events was already assured: James' stubborn foolishness had doomed him and it was too late now to call a free parliament which could arbitrate.

The day after William left Hungerford Irish troops in Reading tried to ambush 350 Dutch soldiers entering the town from the West. The townsfolk managed to warn the Dutch and they avoided the ambush, storming down the Butts, overwhelming James's men in street battles in Broad Street, Market Place and London Street. As the Irish fell back to Twyford the Redingensians feted William's men; James's reliance on Irish (Catholic) regiments did not help engender patriotic support for his cause. At Hungerford William had received an invitation from the University of Oxford and he headed north through Newbury, Farnborough and West Ilsley as far as the neighbourhood of Abingdon. At this same time one of the few reported instances of serious indiscipline by Dutch soldiers took place at East Hendred where they desecrated the chapel at the home of the Eyston family.

Littlecote House, Hungerford.

James pretended to negotiate with William about a free parliament but soon fled from the capital. At Sheerness, when trying to board a ship, he was recognised and forced to return to London where there was still some sympathy for him, but William's Dutch Guard were already masters of the city and judiciously he let James escape to France.

On 27 November James had left Windsor for the last time and on December 14 William entered the castle to remain for four days, 'being lodged in those rooms called Will Chaffinch's and dining above in the king's dining room'. With his confidant and friend Bentinck, later Duke of Portland, he greeted the many noblemen who came to join the obviously winning side but his manner was described as 'grave and cool'. Despite the castle influence the town of Windsor had long been Whig and anti-Court, and William's accession was greeted there with bonfires and 'kilderkins of drink'.

Prospect of Windsor Castle from the south–south-west engraved by Wenceslas Hollar, circa 1660.

He received a communication from James who was at Rochester inviting him to meet him at Whitehall. William's response was a curt instruction to James to remain where he was. At a council of all the peers assembled at Windsor in December it was agreed to ask James to retire, and on the next day the invaders' army marched out for London.

Epilogue – 'Uneasy Lies the Head'

'Dutch William' was described by one biographer as the 'first European'; certainly he had a cosmopolitan inheritance, his great grandparents included James I, Anne of Denmark, Henry IV of France and Marie Medici, and his title and motto: 'je maintaindrai' came from the little principality of Orange, buried in the heart of France itself.

William was a man of subtle restraint but remarkably passionate in his love for his Dutch homeland. In England his spirits were often low and homesickness contributed to his always indifferent health. Soon after his accession to the English throne he observed wistfully: 'The weather is warm now at the Hague, the Kermesse (Carnival) is on. Oh! if only one could fly over there now, just once, like a bird through the air! I would give a hundred guelders, yes, two hundred thousand, just to be there.'

Unexpectedly, his wife Mary, who, when she married him when only fifteen, had at first wept at the prospect before her, not only came to love William but also the meadows and forests and windmills and stolid citizens of her husband's country (and that love was reciprocated). Indeed she and William shared an active continuing interest in their Dutch properties and when William launched his invasion of England she, like Ruth in the Bible, was reluctant to leave her adopted people but would have lived happily in the land of their fathers for ever.

William and Mary's lifestyle in the Netherlands was almost unpretentiously bourgeois when briefly he could be spared from warfaring or was not indulging his passion for hunting, he smoking his pipe and she planting her flowers and both accessible and easy with their fellow countrymen. However, William was an autocrat not a democrat and could be ruthless in sustaining his authority. William was never an effective charmer like his wife's Stuart uncle, and emollient pleasantries were not in his armoury, nor, in general, did he enjoy the society of women as much as men. Bishop Burnet said that William had only 'one (discreet) vice' and it was hinted that he was homosexual, which most historians report only to deny; it is unfair and unfortunate that this has the effect of 'no smoke without fire' and insinuates that this could be a blemish. Mary was a contrast to her husband, taller than him, good-looking with red hair and dark eyes, outgoing where he was reserved, being warm and affectionate and receiving ready affection in return. Her passionate femininity was something which William found it hard to respond to, and there was undoubtedly much domestic unhappiness before they came to appreciate and

A lady tending her tulips in a Dutch formal garden. Queen Mary would have been at home here; gardening was one of her chief delights.

depend on one another's virtues. Of all the kings and queens of England their names are nearly always spoken of together, and their entwined monogram can still be seen in many places.

When James II fled many of his subjects, especially men of influence, were uncertain as to what kind of monarch and monarchy they wished to succeed him. After much debate and after Mary had refused to ascend to the throne alone, Parliament accepted that William and Mary should be joint sovereigns, with William as effective administrator. A Declaration of Rights intended in part to guarantee popular liberties was read to William and Mary for their acceptance prior to their accession. However, many Tories and particularly Anglican clergymen had troubled consciences which prevented them from taking the oath of allegiance stipulated within it. These men known as 'non-jurors' were soon joined by others, some of whom detested the Dutchmen like Bentinck who not unnaturally had the ear of the king whom they had long served. As we have seen a number of the dissatisfied, including Churchill, carried on a hesitant and ineffectual intrigue with the Jacobite exiles in France partly as an insurance policy against an uncertain future.

The Queen's drawing room at Hampton Court was intended by Sir Christopher Wren to be part of a much more lavish building.

One of the first places visited by William when he reached his Capital was the Tudor palace at Hampton Court. The polluted atmosphere of smoky and damp London which engulfed the central palace at Whitehall where it was expected the court would reside was purgatory for the asthmatic king, who thought that rural Hampton Court would prove much more congenial; it was his initial intention to have demolished entirely the existing buildings of Henry VIII's time and erected a royal residence to rival in splendour that at Versailles. Perhaps fortunately, financial constraints prevented Wren who was engaged for the project from eliminating all of the Tudor structure and we are left today to admire the warm west frontage with crenellated parapet and tall chimneys, and an east aspect from William's day, massive and handsome but stolid and austere. Queen Mary was enthusiastically involved in the work, 'giving thereon her own judgment which was exquisite'. As soon as possible their majesties spent most of their time at Hampton Court to the exasperation of courtiers who had to trundle long hours between there and the Capital. 'The King's inaccessibleness and living soe . . . and at soe active a time ruined all the business.'

Wren worked on alterations and adaptations at Hampton Court for William and Mary from 1689–1702. This is the east front.

Nottingham House was bought by William in 1688. The King ordered Wren to enlarge it and this London royal residence became known as Kensington Palace.

To resolve some of these problems William and Mary purchased in 1689 Nottingham House in Kensington, a village that 'esteemed a very good Air'. A new road was built from London through Hyde Park to Kensington, illuminated by lamps for safety, the 'Rue du Roi', Rotten Row. At what became Kensington Palace large-scale extensions were undertaken by Wren, with Hawksmoor as clerk of works, and again Mary 'impatient to be at that place' and the king driving on the masons. Perhaps intimations of her own mortality impelled Mary but, certainly, the haste in part occasioned a serious accident when a section of the house collapsed causing at least one fatality. A similar collapse had occurred at Hampton Court during work there.

Kensington was provided with apartments for the principal courtiers and became the hub of government. Because William and Mary were joint sovereigns both the two palaces had separate apartments and suites for each monarch. Mary's passionate and artistic nature was engaged to produce sumptuous creations indoors and in the gardens where in Kensington:

'Beems from afar a moving tulip-bed,
Where rich brocades and glossy damasks glow,
And chints . . .'

Her death in 1694 precluded her from enjoying some of the most attractive of the new building such as the Queen's Gallery and closet at Hampton Court.

In the years of the 17th century preceding the coming to England of William the Dutch Republic enjoyed a Golden Age of commerce and culture. During this time she was at war with England on several occasions and at others she was in an alliance with her to defend the Protestant faith.

As Trevelyan wrote: 'As friends or enemies, as partners or rivals, men of the two nations were now in perpetual contact. Holland

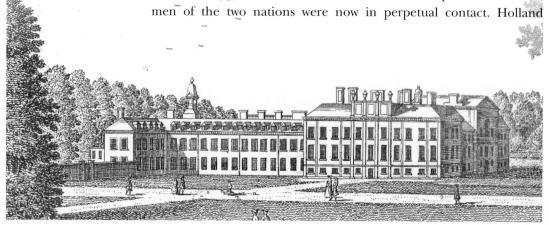

affected every department of English life, more perhaps, than any other nation has ever done by mere force of example. . . . last but not least, the example to our merchants and politicians of a community which had attained prosperity, enlightenment and power by rebellion against a legitimate prince.' The strange English sense of humour has ensured that we retain from those days phrases such as 'Dutch courage', 'Double Dutch' and 'I'm a Dutchman'. And the reign of William and Mary saw Dutch influences increasingly embodied into our culture, from the mighty matters of finance and engineering to the obsessive cultivation of the tulip and its incorporation as a motif in design, and the less happy popularity of cheap (tax-free) gin drinking.

There is no room here to examine the years of William's reign, except to note that soon England would unite with or subsume Ireland and five years after William's death Scotland in a greater 'Great Britain'. In Ireland William becomes the hero of the Ulster protestants (Orangemen) for his victories over James when he attempted to regain his throne through the Catholics of the island; while the bloody massacre of the less-than-innocent branch of the Clan Macdonald in Glencoe is a persistent image used to cast a dark shadow on William's reputation in Scotland.

Many Scots resented discrimination against them by their often grasping and arrogant English neighbours; others looked on the prospect of Union with eager economic anticipation, as Dr Johnson later averred.

'The best-laid plans . . .' Often the simple facts of nature rather than politics fashion our history. Elizabeth's 'barren stock' and childlessness heralded the coming of the Stuarts, and the agonies of miscarriage and early childhood deaths of all their progeny which were the fate of William's Mary and her sister Anne brought us the Hanoverians.

William and Mary's monogram above the garden door on the Queen's side of the Palace.

The English patriotic and religious fervour of Westcountrymen in the two rebellions we have portrayed found a solution to its anxieties in a Dutchman, as earlier and later the continuity of the throne and kingdom was sustained by immigrant claimants from Scotland and from Germany.

William R

Marie R.

People of some importance and influence at work between 1650 and 1710

ARCHITECTS

Nicolas Hawksmoor 1661–1736. Architect who assisted Sir Christopher Wren in various 'Royal Works' and whose later achievements included the chapel and hall at Queen's College, Oxford.

Sir John Vanbrugh 1664–1726. Playwright and architect of Castle Howard and Blenheim Palace.

Sir Christopher Wren 1632–1723. Best-known of all British architects
(see *Sir Christopher Wren*, Michael St John Parker, Wessex Books, 1998)

ARTISTS

Grinling Gibbons 1648–1721. Dutch wood-carver and sculptor highly valued by Wren.

Sir Godfrey Kneller 1645–1723. Born in Germany, the English portrait painter to four monarchs.

Jean Tijou *fl* 1689–1712. A French iron-worker whose work happily matched that of Grinling Gibbons in wood. His screens provided an essential element in many of Wren's compositions.

MUSICIANS

Henry Purcell 1659–95. Musician and composer, 'Keeper of the King's Instruments'.

SCIENTISTS

Robert Boyle 1626–91. Scientist, chemist. Boyle's Law 1662 (volume of a given mass of gas varies universally with the pressure when the temperature is constant). Member of the Royal Society. Pioneered the proper recording of experimental procedures.

Edmund Halley 1656–1742. Astronomer and mathematician, mentor to Isaac Newton, 'Halley's Comet'.

Robert Hooke 1635–1703. Physicist and chemist, Secretary to the Royal Society.

Sir Isaac Newton 1642–1727. Mathematician and 'greatest of all physical scientists', Master of the Mint, MP, President of the Royal Society.

WRITERS

John Aubrey 1626–97. Antiquary and biographer, author of *Brief Lives*.

Aphra Behn 1640–1689. Novelist and playwright, the first woman in England to earn her living as a writer; wrote against slavery.

William Dampier 1651–1715. Skilled seaman, explorer, hydrographic surveyor, rescued Alexander Selkirk (*Robinson Crusoe*).

John Dryden 1631–1700. Poet, satirist, playwright.

John Evelyn 1620–1706. Diarist and provider of major source of information for 66 years.

Celia Fiennes 1662–1741. Her accounts of travels on horseback throughout England in the reigns of James II and William III give a uniquely detailed picture of her time.

Samuel Pepys 1633–1703. Incomparable diarist, Secretary to the Admiralty, 'Saviour of the Navy'.

OTHERS

Elias Ashmole 1617–92. Antiquarian and astrologer (The Ashmolean Museum, Oxford).

William Penn 1644–1718. Quaker and founder of Pennsylvania in 1681 (given as repayment for a debt from Charles II).

Family and place names which were first significant in the Court and aristocracy of this era have a clear resonance in events of today: Bentinck, Buccleuch, Keppel, Spencer and Churchill, and Althorp, Blenheim and Kensington Palace.

In September 1684 the Marquis of Bath bought 1,000 best mixed tulips for £5 and 1,000 second best tulips for £2.50 for planting at Longleat. The tulip was known in the middle east long before it became an obsession with the Dutch but it was there in the early seventeenth century that the stern Calvinist Hollanders let themselves go in the orgy of 'tulipomania', when a single bulb could purchase a dowry or even a brewery! Long before William came to us to be king the tulip was well established here (as well as many things Dutch – engineers to drain the Fens, money to invest in our burgeoning commerce). In the Civil War a royalist commander and flower-grower Sir Thomas Hanmer interrupted the grim proceedings to send tulips to another horticultural enthusiast, the Roundhead General Lambert. As Anna Pavord says in her massive work *The Tulip*: 'throughout the cataclysmic events, the comings and goings of kings and protectors, the Gunpowder Plot, the Plague, the Great Fire, the tulip remained untoppled on its flowery throne'. The tulip became a motif for pottery, marquetry and furnishings (see the Stoke Edith tapestries at Montacute) and after William and Mary ascended the throne their passion for gardening ensured that this emblematic flower became ubiquitous.

Bibliography

Charles II Antonia Fraser (Weidenfeld and Nicolson 1979)

The Dutch Republic Jonathan I Israel (Oxford 1995)

Dynasty of the Stuarts John Macleod (Hodder and Stoughton 1999)

History of England Thomas Babington, Lord Macaulay (Longman Green 1889)

Sir Christopher Wren Michael St John Parker (Wessex Books 1998)

England Under The Stuarts G M Trevelyan (Folio Society 1996)

Samuel Pepys, The Unequalled Self Claire Tomalin (Viking 2002)

The Prince It Is That's Come Joy Packe (Tre Kemynyon 1984)

1688 Revolution In The Family Henry and Barbara van der Zee (Viking 1988)

Ungrateful Daughters Maureen Waller (Hodder & Stoughton 2002)

The Western Rising Charles Chevenix Trench (Longman 1969)

William and Mary Henry and Barbara van der Zee (Macmillan 1988)

Acknowledgements

All pictures in this book are from the author's private collection, except for the following, for use of which the publishers gratefully thank:

Local people, libraries, museums and galleries have been very helpful in the preparation of this book and we are grateful to them.

Prof. Fred G.H. Bachrach, p.2, p.31, cover panel (bottom);

British Library, ifc;

R. Drake, p.22, p.35 top;

Fitzwilliam Museum, p.47;

C. and H, Grimley, p.34 bottom;

Tom Hazelhurst, p.4 bottom;

Andrew Jamieson, cover border.

A.F. Kersting ABIPP FRPS, p.42, p.43;

Marquess of Bath, p.7;

Mary Evans Picture Library, p.4 top, p.30 top;

Christopher Nicolson, p.19 (inset);

Geoff Roberts Photography, p.27;

The Royal Collection, p.30 bottom;

Somerset Archaeological and Natural History Society, p.8, p.12, p.14, p.16, p.18, p.21, p.23, p.24;

Michael Stirling, p.6 top, p.19, front cover panel;

Text © Douglas F. Stuckey

Designed and edited by Jane Drake

Design © Wessex Books 2004

Published by Wessex Books 2004

Printed by Thruxton Press Ltd

ISBN 1-903035-21-X